Washington: Seasons of the Capital

DATE DUE			

*To my parents for letting me follow my inspiration, and
to my wife for continuing to inspire.*—P.A.

*For Mary who married me in Georgetown on the first
day of fall, and for Tim who arrived in Foggy Bottom
on the verge of spring.*—P.K.

*Cover: The dome of the Capitol and towers of the Smithsonian
Institution Building rise from a sea of leaves and cherry blossoms.
Page 1: An archway frames white azaleas in a corner of
Dumbarton Oaks.
Pages 4-5: The summer dusk lingers as a cyclist pedals her way
past Memorial Bridge.
Pages 6-7: Early autumn shows its colors between the spires of
Georgetown University and the Potomac River boathouses.
Pages 8-9: In winter the Reflecting Pool mirrors an image of the
Washington Monument—with the Capitol to its left in the distance,
and the Library of Congress and the Smithsonian "Castle" to its right.
Pages 10-11: In springtime a field of daffodils borders the Potomac,
perfect place for a lovers' picnic.*

Designed by Rebecca K. McClimans
Edited by Carolyn M. Clark
Photography © 1992 by Ping Amranand. All rights reserved.
Text © 1992 by Philip Kopper. All rights reserved.
© 1992 by Elliott & Clark Publishing. All rights reserved.
This book, or any portions thereof, may not be reproduced in any
form without written permission of the publisher.
Printed and bound in Hong Kong by Palace Press
Any inquiries should be directed to Elliott & Clark Publishing,
P.O. Box 21365, Washington, DC 20009,
Telephone (202) 387-9805

Library of Congress Cataloging-in-Publication Data
Amranand, Ping.
   Washington: seasons of the capital / photography by Ping Amranand
;history by Philip Kopper.
      p. cm.
   ISBN 1-880216-08-6
   1. Seasons—Washington (D.C.)—Pictorial works. 2. Seasons—
Washington (D.C.)—History. 3. Washington (D.C.)—Pictorial works.
4. Washington (D.C.)—History. I. Kopper, Philip. II. Title.
F195.A546 1992
975.3—dc20   92-38747
                                                   CIP

WASHINGTON

Seasons of the Capital

PHOTOGRAPHY BY PING AMRANAND

HISTORY BY PHILIP KOPPER

ELLIOTT & CLARK PUBLISHING

WASHINGTON, D.C.

Preamble: Looking Backward

Even in winter two centuries after the city was founded, water stays essential to Washington's look and character. The frozen Reflecting Pool shows that plain enough, as the three other introductory photographs prove a kindred point: this capital arose on the Potomac, which in those days provided a sure means for travel, transport, commerce, and communication. A city without a river could hardly function, let alone lead a nation out of infancy.

Much of Washington's modern beauty reflects its origins, as the obelisk commemorates the capital's name-giver or the Capitol dome and Smithsonian "Castle" remind that this city was endowed with complex purposes at its birth. Like a princess born into a noble house or a cad in a Gothic novel, this city entered the world with its role in life already defined and its rank declared. The city's essence was indelibly asserted in its charter and engraved in its original plan.

Here was no city-state rudely paled by wolf-nursed twins nor medieval market town grown beyond the banks of its river-moated isle. In the most rational of both English and Enlightenment traditions, it was planned. Furthermore, it was sited by an act of politics. Intended to head an ambitious nation, it was chosen, designed, mapped, and platted to suit its premier role. Many aspects of that role—of its urban and urbane character—were declared at the time of founding, while others came hand in glove.

The capital was not just a federal center, the place for legislators to gather and governors to sit. According to the dictates of that time, which in turn were inherited and modified by every generation since, it must also become a place of civility and amenities. This government seat would nurture a city of learning in the sciences and arts, a capital of culture and of commerce. Especially as it reflected the tenets of its changing times it would be a city of enduring beauty and growing grandeur, at least in its formal precincts—our only focus in these pages.

Beneath the painted magnificence of the Capitol Rotunda stands the likeness of Roger Williams, founder of the Rhode Island colony in 1636, one of ninety-five statues of prominent citizens donated to the Capitol by the fifty states.

Inspired in part by Louis XIV's Versailles and Christopher Wren's plan for London, the capital city was equally intended as a locus for contemplation, recreation, and culture. John Adams, the first president to inhabit the White House, declared that he must study politics and war so that his sons could practice commerce, science, and industry, so that their sons might learn literature, music, and art. These were the goals of Humanism as the eighteenth century turned, the ideals of worthy men when the Federal city was founded. Thus Washington himself died in 1799, and in 1800, Washington, D.C., was born.

Years per se have different meanings here: odd-numbered ones are less important than even, and leap years bear the crown because they ring in elections that bring new players to the government arena, new denizens to town. After three decades in Washington, I know the coming-round-again of January 1 rarely matters for its own sake; the tides in the affairs of men rise and fall in longer cycles. Rather it is the changing of the times of year—the portions within the twelvemonth—that reassure and surprise delightfully. The Senate floor rarely sees fireworks to match those along the C & O Canal when the leaves turn in autumn. Nor have I heard a political wind blow as clear as a northern gale blasting across the Mall and whipping the constant ring of flags around the monument into a snapping frenzy. In Washington, as years fade one into another, it is the changing seasons that we cheer and cherish.

Beginnings: The City of Springtime

I f spring is the season of promise and subtle stirring, Washington's springtime lasted ages before its pace quickened and the Federal era opened. Here the edge of a rich coastal plain nestled against the first foothills of old mountains, and a brawny river cut its way through bedrock to sprawl between marshy banks below the cataracts. Here in a region inhabited for a thousand years, canny Algonquins fished the rich tidewaters in dugout canoes, burned off forest undergrowth to nurture browse for game (which caused a parklike beauty that enticed English explorers), and traveled natural routes over land and water to trade with distant native nations. Here the tide-swelled Potomac ran deep enough to bear the newcomers' ships as far up as the falls, thus enabling an inland outpost that offered the comforts of access to the rest of colonial America and mother Europe. Here, by the time the Continental Congress liberated thirteen colonies, two of the new "free and independent states" shared a boundary, so that this river had two votes in any contest over the choice of a site for the promised capital of the new nation. In sum, what lay here was a

vibrant, alluring, spectacular convergence of natural assets, human resources, and political possibilities.

Springtime 1791 brought the man who conceived the actual city as it would appear in streets and stones. That March a French artist-turned-engineer, Pierre Charles L'Enfant, began riding day by day through dense, dripping woods and rolling farms between two tributaries of the Potomac to study how the land lay. He declared no area "in America can be more susceptible to grand improvement" than the stretch between the Eastern Branch (now the Anacostia River) and the Potomac at Georgetown, an expanse owned by barely twenty families whose plantations ran from a few hundred acres to a few thousand.

Son of an aristocratic painter in the Court of Versailles, L'Enfant had been an art student at the Royal Academy in Paris fifteen years earlier when he followed the Marquis de Lafayette across the Atlantic. Joining the English colonists' rebellion, he had illustrated Baron von Steuben's training manuals, led a charge, and distinguished himself as a builder of earthen fortifications. Captain L'Enfant was wounded in battle, captured by the

Daffodils rise among a Capitol Hill garden's handpicked rocks and random petals.
Opposite: The Jefferson Memorial looms in the rain beyond the Tidal Basin ringed with cherry trees—Washington's triumph of spring.

British, swapped for a Hessian, commissioned a major, and decorated by his king, Louis XVI. He was singled out by General Washington who, after the war, chose him to design the emblems for his fraternity of officers, the Society of the Cincinnati. In New York he won a reputation as an architect among influential gentlemen and was chosen to design Congress' new meeting place in Federal Hall, making it the most elegant building in the temporary capital city and one that pleased all in every detail except its cost.

Meanwhile the ineffectual Articles of Confederation had been superseded by the Constitution, and George Washington was now the president of a stronger central government. The thorny question of where that government would sit permanently had been answered in a compromise (or horse-trade if you like) struck by diametric political geniuses, the yeoman's champion from Virginia, Thomas Jefferson, and the New York dandy, Alexander Hamilton. The Secretary of State and Secretary of the Treasury agreed that the new nation's capital would rise somewhere below the Mason-Dixon Line—to the lasting honor of Jefferson's South. In return, the new federal government would shoulder any state's Revolutionary War debts—to the immediate financial relief of Hamilton's North.

Congress left it to Washington himself to locate the capital city, and he selected "a situation not excelled for commanding prospect, good water, salubrious air and safe harbour by any in the world." The chosen district

The Enid A. Haupt Garden makes a seasonal carpet behind the many-towered "Castle," designed by James Renwick as the Smithsonian Institution's original building, which opened in 1855.

A statue of Justice flanks the steps of the Supreme Court. Nearby the Library of Congress' Jefferson Building boasts a torch of learning atop its cupola. Inset and opposite: A Muse adorns the 1890s Beaux Arts Jefferson Building that features a spectacularly round main reading room.

embraced the head of navigation on the Potomac, the infant tobacco port of Georgetown on the eastern shore, and, on the western, the bustling town of Alexandria hard by his own plantation. (Neither Mount Vernon nor its abundantly rich master would suffer from the proximity.) Virginia and Maryland ceded the lands in question and a 100-square-mile diamond was designated, its corners pointing in the cardinal directions at Jefferson's inspiration.

Many new towns in eighteenth-century America were laid out in advance—witness Annapolis, Maryland's second capital, and Williamsburg, Virginia's capital before Richmond. The nation's proposed new seat

would be no exception, and L'Enfant lobbied slavishly for this commission to build a city on farmland and forest ground. As he wrote to President Washington, "Sir: The late determination of Congress to lay the foundation of a city which is to become the capital of this vast empire offers so great an occasion of acquiring reputation to whoever may be appointed...that your Excellency will not be surprised that my ambition and the desire I have of becoming a useful citizen should lead me to wish to share in the undertaking." He wanted the job, and Washington felt lucky awarding it to him, the comrade in arms he admired as an engineer who augmented "professional knowledge" with "considerable

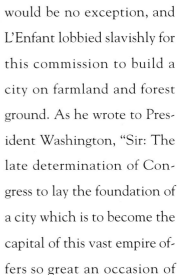

taste." The president later wrote, "for prosecuting public works and carrying them into effect, [L'Enfant] was better qualified than any one who had come within my knowledge in this country."

President Washington and Secretary of State Jefferson bade L'Enfant to plan a capital that would rival Paris in magnificence (though its vocabulary echoed Roman antiquity. For example, a local planter named Francis Pope had called his acres "Rome" and gave as grand a name to its largest stream when he christened plain old Goose Creek the "Tiber.") L'Enfant responded with a plan "on such a scale as to leave room for that *aggrandizement and embellishment* which the increase of the wealth of the nation will permit it to pursue at any period however remote." [Italics added.] In short, the French visionary set himself the task of designing for the ages.

L'Enfant arrived in a springtime watered by "an heavy rain and thick mist... [which] does put an insuperable obstacle to my wish of proceeding immediately." When the weather moderated and he began quartering the district owned by a tight-knit and much intermarried squirearchy, dogwoods and shadbush would be bursting into bloom, punctuating the greening forests with swatches of pink and white. But this surveyor was less interested in botany than in the natural features of the land. He was looking for dominant sites to anchor his idealized arrangement of urban amenities that would both captivate heirs of the Enlightenment and inspire exponents of the new democracy.

His plan for the "federal city" reflected the shape of the government's organization. The Presidential Palace (as L'Enfant regally called it), would rise on a broad plain over-

Azaleas and dogwoods bloom profusely in a wooded glen at the U.S. National Arboretum. Right: A pink dogwood tree stands sentry among the identical gravestones at Arlington National Cemetery.

looking Tiber Creek and the Potomac. The coequal Congress House would surmount the promontory called Jenkins Hill which he deemed "a pedestal waiting for a monument" in a letter to his patron. (A bit of a toady, L'Enfant wanted to name the city "Washingtonople.")

As for access between these two poles, he ordered the channeling of Tiber Creek into a canal; thus when a President wished to call upon the national legislature, he might travel by the Presidential Barge. Moreover, Palace and Capitol would be joined by the city's principal boulevard, Pennsylvania Avenue, which L'Enfant emphasized by extending it all the way to Georgetown in the west and to the Eastern Branch of the Potomac. (No matter that the Tiber frequently flooded this main street and that Rock Creek's valley remained an unbridged chasm; posterity could address those matters.)

Why *Pennsylvania* Avenue? Some historians think it was a consolation prize to that state, though more likely the honor resulted from the accident of symbolic proximity: thirteen of the city's avenues were named for the original states in a rough northwest-to-southeast sequence that reflected their relative geographic positions north to south. (In checking this today, remember that L'Enfant's plan for the federal city covered only a fraction of the District of Columbia's 100-square-mile territory—from the rivers up to the arcing Boundary Street [present-day Florida Avenue]. Also note that Georgia Avenue originally ran past Congressional Cemetery in the city's

The large, many-windowed addition to the old Willard Hotel offers a dark contrast to the golden, neoclassical Department of the Treasury Building.

southeast quadrant before this street was re-named Potomac Avenue, and "Georgia" was appropriated for the avenue piercing the city's northern apex.)

Hampered by neither timidity nor doubt, L'Enfant accepted the commission to design both the city and its major buildings. Indeed, he would willingly stop at nothing to achieve his majestic conception—and this determination was his Achilles heel. When he came upon a substantial brick house being built by a leader of the gentry where a boulevard was planned, L'Enfant had it razed. He simply knocked the mansion down in one of a thousand acts of hubris that cost him dearly.

Pierre L'Enfant had a fertile imagination, as some of his unrealized plans best suggest. At the foot of Jenkins Hill he planned a "grand Avenue...400 feet in breadth, and about a mile in length, bordered with gardens." Stretching to the Potomac, it would be lined with the estates of foreign embassies and the grandest mansions in the city. Leading down

Now a museum, Hillwood preserves the luxury that cereal heiress Marjorie Merriweather Post created when she built a mansion adorned with art and gardens. Above: Orchids and other exotic plants flourish in the U.S. Botanic Garden at the foot of Capitol Hill. Pages 26-27: The Bishop's Garden, one of special serenity, graces the Washington National Cathedral on Mount Saint Alban.

Capitol Hill to that avenue he imagined an artificial waterfall draining into the Tiber canal. Nearby, he mandated a "pantheon," a national shrine for religious services. But more important than these castles in the air is the manifold legacy that he created in fact.

In barely a year L'Enfant conceived a plan and began laying out a city that could boast remarkable variety in street patterns,

For every house a gardener, it seems: in the neighborhood called Cleveland Park (since President Cleveland spent his summers here) wisteria cascades the length of a veranda. Opposite: A Georgetowner's tiny acreage sprouts tulips.

block sizes, and vistas—the heart of a metropolis that would rise slowly out of rustic wilderness. He borrowed ideas from sources as close as Jefferson's notebook, as distant as Christopher Wren's plan for London, and as grandiose as the Sun King Louis XIV's Versailles, his own boyhood home. He blended these devices into an original plan that could grow and change as the nation matured.

Once L'Enfant found sites for the preeminent buildings to house the President and Congress, he superimposed a conventional grid of east-west and north-south streets,

which Jefferson had suggested, designating them alphabetically and numerically as the city's commissioners ordered. But grids get tedious, and he relieved this one by slanting avenues across the regular pattern, creating starbursts of odd-angled, many-pointed intersections where the boulevards crossed byways. In these polygonal intersections he drew circles, squares, oblongs, triangles in a mélange of sizes, shapes, and purposes—some for squares to honor the states, others for monuments, ceremonial entrances, or placid parks. These, along with the varied and extravagant widths of thoroughfares, gave the city its unique character, a fact as apparent at the dawn of the nineteenth century as it remains in the dusk of the twentieth.

Much, however, did not go L'Enfant's way. A gifted designer and synthesist, he was arrogant and intransigent. As a diplomat he had no tact, as a negotiator he leapt for the ultimatum; as a political animal, *L'Enfant* was simply *terrible*. When an auction to sell house lots was scheduled to raise funds for laying streets and public buildings, he refused to disclose his plan's details in vain hope of deterring speculators. Making dictatorial decisions about routes and building sites, he quickly managed to anger the city's commissioners, offend its landowners, and alienate most other people with clout. Later, when a benefactor offered him a teaching post at West Point, he turned it down as a sinecure beneath his dignity. When President Washington offered him $2,500 and a house site in the city as grateful

A brisk wind displays the flags surrounding the Washington Monument—and a telephoto lens brings the mile-and-a-quarter-distant Capitol close—as a spring day lures tourists and locals to the Mall.

compensation for services rendered, he kissed off the offer and went on to claim that the government owed him sums approaching an astronomical $100,000.

By the time spring came round again in March of 1792, the Secretary of State was writing to L'Enfant: "I am instructed by the President to inform you that notwithstanding the desire he has entertained to preserve your agency...your services must be at an end." He was gone, fired from his job within a year. He had not even gotten to sign the first published map of the city, which showed features evidently added by others, as his plan instantly began to evolve and take on a life of its own.

L'Enfant found lesser work and more conflict elsewhere, then returned to the federal city, his magnum opus. A muttering eccentric with a mangy dog at his heel, he haunted Congress, pressing inflated claims until his death in 1825, by then a pauper living on the generosity of friends. He was buried on a host's plantation a few miles from the city—not quite in potter's field—where he lay for nearly a century before his remains were removed to ground reserved for heroes at Arlington National Cemetery.

It was spring again, May of 1800, when the Federal establishment began arriving in the new city within the District of Columbia — a corps of 131 civil servants, all working for five departments: State, Post Office, Navy, War, and Treasury. The city itself was of a like magnitude. There were 109 brick buildings and 263 wooden ones large enough to inventory. Some 5,000 people lived in the established municipalities, Alexandria and Georgetown, while another 3,000 were scattered throughout the 100 square miles. By 1804 it was yet only a potential metropolis, as one Robert Sutcliffe wrote with tongue in cheek: "We only need here houses, cellars, kitchens, scholarly men, amiable women and

a few other such trifles, to possess a perfect city. In a word, this is the best city in the world to live in—in the future." And so, arguably, it would come to be.

Two centuries ago spring brought the shad up the Potomac and its tributaries, as it does today when fishermen crowd the banks of Rock Creek's tributaries with nets and lines. Two centuries ago laurel and dogwood brightened the native forests, as they now adorn woods and gardens. Sturgeon no longer school up the Potomac to spawn as once they did, but neither did those days see the spectacle surrounding Jefferson's memorial in spring when cherry trees burst into clouds of palest pink, sometimes for nearly a week, sometimes barely lasting days to make the sight more precious. At the peak of spring one year in living memory, the cherries billowed into bloom when a dry and sudden gale snatched the flowers from the branches—and their petals blanketed the surface of the Tidal Basin from edge to edge like a tribute to some Elysian hero. The vision of blossom-laden water lasted only hours until the flowers faded with a falling tide.

Now, as then, the rarest adornments and embellishments (to borrow L'Enfant's terms) are often found in surprising places, especially in spring, even in this city with its galaxies of flowers. You see, if every particular was not included in L'Enfant's Plan, what eventually arose was somehow according to plan. If as the twig is bent so grows the branch, then as the plan is sketched so arises a capital city.

A wave crests and gulls perpetually glide at the Navy Marine Memorial on the west bank of the Potomac.

Pages 36-37: Built to house the Departments of State, War, and Navy, the Executive Office Building now provides offices for people who serve the executive branch.

Growth and Confusion: The Summer City

Washington's metaphoric springtime faded into a summer that lasted much of the nineteenth century, perhaps fittingly since summer in these latitudes of locust trees and honeysuckle seems an endless season of sporadic, unkempt, tangled growth. This is a climate where only trampled ground stays bare, where grass and weeds make carpets overnight, where puddles breed mosquitoes, and trees grow several feet a year racing skeins of vines to reach the sunlight. From the beginning the federal city in summer was torpid, hot, and dusty—except when rain turned the dirt streets to bogs. When it rained hard, the Tiber (née Goose Creek) flooded; Jefferson once helped rescue a man who climbed a tree to escape the rising torrent. L'Enfant's canal replaced much of the Tiber in 1807, not to float a Presidential Barge but to carry freight and serve the often pestilential purpose of an open sewer. Better things were in the offing but they were some time germinating.

For example, at the start of every summer in the late twentieth century there comes a day when the setting sun hangs above the Virginia hills, blazes straight down the westbound streets, and flares in the eyes of every rush-hour driver heading home. This briefly blinding experience proves the city's neat alignment, and lovelier proof lies in the appearance of buildings along K Street: about the time of the summer solstice, jutting doorways or signs and numbers in relief are all sunlit, while the facades themselves stand in shadow—because the buildings stand perfectly parallel to the sun's rays, because the city's grid is precisely aligned upon the surface of the earth.

Two centuries after the creation this alignment proves one secret of Washington's success: call it the fruits of piecemeal cooperation. Call it the ripening of a real city. Setting the federal district's ten-mile square on its corner rather than on its side was Jefferson's idea. The work of accurately placing the square fell to Andrew Ellicott, a surveyor who had laid part of the Mason-Dixon line, and Benjamin Banneker, a self-taught astronomer of remarkable ability and the Black American whose achievements convinced Jefferson that Africans were not inferior. (Ellicott was also the man who apparently altered and certainly signed the first printed map of L'Enfant's plan

East of the Capitol, summer trees shade its ample grounds. Inset: Foliage almost hides the Arts & Industries Building, which was erected to display exhibits salvaged from the Philadelphia Exposition celebrating the nation's centennial.

Outside and in, Union Station displays grandly classical motifs. Opened in 1907, it could accommodate 100,000 people. The station gradually fell into disrepair, neglected until the roof started falling in and pigeons nested inside. In 1988, after a splendid restoration, it reopened as a busy depot and mall.

after the Frenchman was sent packing.) Between them, Ellicott and Banneker found the federal city's bounds, which involved locating the District on maps and marking the ten-mile boundaries on the ground with a series of forty stones, many of which survive still.

One motive for the surveyors' precision involved a national ambition: the new republic intended that the principal meridian of its new capital, the line running down Sixteenth Street and through the President's House, would replace the Greenwich meridian as the international norm for worldwide measurement and navigation. It did not. During the growth and maturation of Washington, much that was intended never happened, much that was planned was delayed, and much that was unexpected came to pass anyway. (Thus, the part of the District on the Potomac's west bank was given back to Virginia and became Arlington, by and large.)

In the early years, Washington remain-

ed countryside dotted with clusters of buildings lacking fences and gardens. A visitor wrote home that the city had no business or industry: "The people are poor, and as far as I can judge, they live like fishes by eating each other." Another visitor recorded: "Except some houses uniformly built, with some public-houses, and here and there a little grog shop, this boasted [Pennsylvania] Avenue is as much wilderness as Kentucky. Some half-starved cattle browsing among the bushes present a melancholy spectacle to the stranger, whose expectation has been warmed up by illusive descriptions of speculative writers. So very thinly is the city populated that quails and other birds are constantly shot within a hundred yards of the capitol."

A decade later, bounties were offered for the stray swine and geese that roamed the streets. Even then a French traveler complained: "There is a constant uproar, the reason for which is that the inhabitants all own

Where L'Enfant imagined a Grand Avenue lined with mansions, the Mall came to be bordered largely by Smithsonian museums that he could not have imagined. Ranging along the north (left) side, from near to far: the National Museum of American History; National Museum of Natural History; National Gallery of Art, West Building; and National Gallery of Art, East Building. On the south (right) side: the Department of Agriculture; Freer Gallery of Art; Smithsonian Institution Building; Arts & Industries Building; Hirschhorn Museum and Sculpture Garden; and National Air & Space Museum.

Skylights for an underground restaurant pierce the plaza between John Russell Pope's original 1937 National Gallery of Art building and I. M. Pei's East Building. Opposite: Kiosks mark the entrance to the Arthur M. Sackler Gallery, part of the Smithsonian's largely subterranean S. Dillon Ripley International Quadrangle.

cows and pigs but not stables. The nocturnal wanderings of these beasts create an awful racket in which they are joined by dogs and cats." When novelist Charles Dickens saw Washington as late as 1842, he described "spacious avenues that begin in nothing and lead nowhere; streets, miles long that only want houses, roads, and inhabitants; public buildings that need but a public to be complete; and ornaments of great thoroughfares, which only lack great thoroughfares to ornament.... It is sometimes called the City of Magnificent Distances, but might be termed with greater propriety the City of Magnificent Intentions."

It did not help that in the third summer of the War of 1812 the British had marched on Washington from the rear (evading ample riverside defenses), captured the city, and burned public buildings including the Capitol, President's House, and Navy Yard. Nor did it help that Congress periodically considered relocating the capital, preferably westward to the middle of the expanding nation. Nonetheless, despite discomfort and much maligning, more people continued coming to Washington than left. Each ten-year census showed the city's population growing steadily all through the nineteenth century and the first six decades of the twentieth (steadily, that is, except during wars; then it spiked).

What did help was the distant death of James Smithson in Genoa in the summer of 1829 and his beau geste, one example of a lucky stroke that would give synergism to the city. A wellborn English dilettante, bachelor, and scientist, James Smithson bequeathed his princely fortune "to found at Washington, under the name Smithsonian Institution, an Establishment for the increase and diffusion of knowledge among men." Here from the hands of a stranger who had not even visited America was an "aggrandizement" that L'Enfant could never have foreseen. Yet it was the sort of "embellishment" that his plan anticipated, enabled, and ennobled.

Smithson and L'Enfant were kindred spirits, even collaborators, though they never met. The cantankerous designer intended a plan that would accommodate an ever greater city "at any period however remote." The eccentric scientist endowed an institution with such a vague mandate that it would have to invent its own purposes and become a font

The original Corcoran
Gallery building was to
be demolished when
Mrs. John F. Kennedy
led a campaign to save
Lafayette Park and its
surroundings; the build-
ing was rescued and
renamed Renwick
Gallery for its designer.
Opposite: Yellow roses
climb a wall beside the
British Ambassador's
residence on Embassy
Row, which ranges along
Massachusetts Avenue.

of culture, learning, art, and science. The one man, commissioned by the government, and the other, acting as a private citizen, offered visions that became posterity's standards. They limned a remarkable way despite the miserable conditions that prevailed for decades in the once and future capital (and despite assorted horrors found in enclaves that still diminish this and every American city).

Washington did grow, of course, and flourish, and become aggrandized and embellished with great buildings, charming vistas, handsome memorials, vigorous forums, and benevolent institutions. These eventualities did not eclipse the nightmares of urban life, yet they made manifest part of the dreams imagined by the fathers (and godfathers) of city and nation. If L'Enfant was as headstrong as a delinquent, his seminal plan proved to have magnificent potential. If Smithson's largess had vague purposes, it led to concrete results and became a model for other philanthropists and institutions. (No matter that his bequest of a fortune was nearly refused by Congressmen who thought America too proud or fearful to accept gifts from strangers.) In the summer of 1838, his gift of £107,960 in gold sovereigns was shipped to the Philadelphia mint, melted down, and sent to Washington as coin of the Republic worth $508,318.

It was another decade before the Smithsonian Institution was organized. Then young James Renwick was hired to design what Con-

gress ordered as its "suitable building, of plain and durable materials and structure, without unnecessary ornament...for the reception and arrangement, upon a liberal scale, of objects of natural history,...a chemical laboratory, a gallery of art." What they got was a fantasy in red sandstone, a multitowered Romanesque castle unlike any other building in town and few elsewhere in the world. It was also a powerful, palpable symbol of private generosity forged into a partnership with the national government—the kind of chance cooperation that would embellish and adorn Washington thereafter.

With the government architecturally anchored by the two poles that L'Enfant sited, the city's surroundings grew piecemeal with the spreading of neighborhood clusters and the erection of building after building to serve a private or eleemosynary or practical purpose. There were great teaching institutions; the first, Georgetown College (later University),

opened its doors to a handful of students in 1791. In 1820, just beyond the federal city's pale of Boundary Street (later Florida Avenue) came Columbian College, as George Washington University was first known. In 1857, a school was founded that became Gallaudet University, the nation's premiere school for the deaf, and in 1864, a college for freed men that became a citadel of higher

learning for blacks, Howard University.

There were ancillary elements of government, such as the Library of Congress, which was destroyed by the British and arose from the ashes with the purchase of Jefferson's personal library. There was the Patent Office, which was nearly torched in 1814 but saved by the Capitol's architect, William Thornton, who (legend says) threw himself across a cannon's bore to protect what he declaimed as "the repository of the inventive genius of America." There would be private organizations like the National Geographic Society

Red tile roofs mark buildings of the Federal Triangle, begun in the 1920s. In the '90s, the last remaining site, the parking lot at lower left, was cleared for development. Above: Vaquero by Louis Jiminez bucks outside of the National Museum of American Art, once the Patent Office Building.

that benefitted from (and contributed to) a growing community of scientists in government and the Smithsonian. There was the American Institute of Architects which set up shop before the Civil War for the specific purpose of being in the nation's capital. There would be the august private museums, starting with W. W. Corcoran's decision to endow his art collection in a building designed by Smithsonian architect James Renwick.

In growing numbers there were ambassadors sent to represent their governments, though many foreign ministries considered Washington a hardship post because of the climate. By June in the face of summer's heat, the federal establishment hunkered down like a hound under the porch. Presidents as early as Martin van Buren in the 1830s vacated the feverish federal city for cooler, healthier outlying precincts of the District. Neighborhoods such as Cleveland Park, Potomac Palisades, and eventually Chevy Chase all began as recreational retreats. By late in the century, summer became the season when all of Washington fled for cooler hustings as far off as Newport, Rhode Island, called the summer capital for its population of warm-weather senators. (In the 1940s, the advent of air conditioning enabled government officials to stay at their desks all year long—and just work more mischief, as critics carped. It was then that governing America became a year-round affair.)

The "magnificient intentions" Dickens saw were not always in vain, though they

Once the home of orator John C. Calhoun and later of diplomat Robert Bliss, Dumbarton Oaks is now an art museum, study center, and public garden. In summer, the gardens look formal and lush with boxwood and assorted annuals.

often took time to realize. For instance, private donations were collected to erect a towering obelisk on the site that L'Enfant intended for George Washington's equestrian statue, and in 1848, the cornerstone was laid. Six years later the stump reached 153 feet, money ran out, and work stopped. It was stalled for a generation until Congress funded completion of the Washington Monument's last four-fifths, a task that proceeded at 50 feet a year until the tallest structure in the world topped out in 1888 at 555 feet.

Perseverance could be impressive, as when the cast-iron dome of the Capitol was completed during the Civil War. This was an enormous engineering project at the time, and military priorities suggested tabling it. But President Lincoln insisted on its completion as a symbol of the Union that the war was waged to preserve—a war, incidentally, that nearly destroyed the city which was invaded only by friendly troops. Around the stump of the Washington Monument, for example, corrals held hundreds of thousands of horses and cattle—stock for teamsters and meat on the hoof for the quartermaster. Meanwhile there were soldiers billeted in the Capitol and sick

and wounded lying in makeshift hospitals all over town. The city had never known quite such drama, which peaked with the tragedy of Lincoln's murder and the anticlimax of the days-long Grand Review when the armies of the Union paraded up Pennsylvania Avenue. Like other streets in the city, it had been worn by the traffic of troops and military materiel; now its paving was broken so badly that merchants gave up proud addresses and moved.

Dedicated in 1942, the Jefferson Memorial stands on a manmade island overlooking the Tidal Basin, an engineer's invention of the 1880s. Filled twice daily by the rising tide, the Basin empties via its downstream outlet to prevent Washington Channel from silting up. Right: The Channel serves pleasure boats and the thriving Maine Avenue seafood market. Pages 54-55: Seen from a balustrade along Rock Creek Parkway is Memorial Bridge, which leads to Arlington National Cemetery below the Custis-Lee Mansion.

The city nearly doubled its population between 1860 and 1870 to 132,000 souls, and this influx brought new pressures to bear. Local government had been thoroughly confused for years because a board of commissioners governed the federal city while the rural reach beyond Boundary Street was overseen by a court. In any case, with the coming of peace to the nation, the capital entered a

The Capitol dome sends a message to all in sight: Congress is not in session—as indicated by the lack of a light in the cupola. Opposite: The floodlit facade of the White House silhouettes Andrew Jackson's statue in Lafayette Park, the first equestrian statue erected in Washington.

kind of gravid state as if the fruit of its long summer's growth were about to burst forth. The rest of the nation turned to peacetime pursuits, and Washington gained territorial status, i.e., the limited self-government that elsewhere in the Republic led to statehood. Now, with the stage set for another leap in urbane identity, enter Alexander R. Shepherd.

A big, hearty man with a big, loud laugh, Shepherd strode about this scene of teeming, tangled fertility like a Jolly Green Giant. He was a local boy, born in 1835 in the southwest neighborhood called the Island, one of a lum-

berman's several children. Sent to work at the age of ten, he was a successful plumber and building contractor by the time the Civil War broke out; he was rich by the time peace came between the states. Shepherd was the first to specialize in building homes for people of modest means, which meant row houses for government workers, a corps that continued to grow at a reliable rate and increased his fortune accordingly.

When the District of Columbia gained the status of a territory, its government began to grow, then to swell. A glad-hander with a ready wit, Shepherd was popular with macho men, among them the rough-cut President Grant who named him to the Board of Public Works. Soon he dominated that body, and in so doing became the most important man in town. Shepherd resembled the aloof L'Enfant in that he set out to do things his own way, and the devil take the hindmost. In fact, he would do more to shape the city than any single man since L'Enfant's time. Swinging a wrecker's maul, he set Washington on its feet: witness Liberty Market, a hotchpotch of open stalls near today's Mount Vernon Square. Shepherd meant to replace and update it, but the merchants refused to vacate, and so one night he sent in a gang of workmen who razed it before dawn. When a railroad defied him by blocking Pennsylvania Avenue with a stalled locomotive, Shepherd removed the tracks fore and aft to strand the engine.

An earlier mayor who timidly paved a few streets had cut the extraordinary cost of

paving L'Enfant's extraordinarily wide thoroughfares by narrowing them with ample "parking." (This term then did not mean a place to leave a vehicle; it meant a border of grass and/or trees beside a carriageway—like a park, hence "parking.") Shepherd borrowed the trick and applied it with abandon. Within eighteen months he paved 118 miles of streets plus 39 miles of outlying roads straight through long stretches of farms and woodland to the borders of the District.

Drainage had always been a problem in the federal city; he solved it by regrading the entire central area so that a workable sewer system could be built. Suddenly the flooding of the streets was no longer a seasonal occurrence. But wholesale regrading left some houses twenty feet above the new street level and some barely visible as a new grade rose around them. When householders, even Congressmen, complained of damage to the foundations, he ordered them to secure their houses or see them demolished at their own expense. Shepherd filled in L'Enfant's canal to end a major health hazard. He installed gas lines to bring new lighting (and new habits) to the leisured. He installed trolley tracks which altered how people traveled to work, enabling more people to commute and to commute farther.

Not everyone approved, especially old-line residents, as Shepherd spent his au-

Milestones of flight hang suspended in the Smithsonian's National Air & Space Museum, reportedly the most popular museum in the world.
Above: A few miles uptown at another Smithsonian adjunct, the National Zoological Park, a bamboo meal preoccupies one of the famous giant pandas given by the People's Republic of China.

thorized budget several times over; his spending even exceeded what had been spent in the city's entire previous history. Congress investigated three times and determined that he was as straight with tax money as he was devious in his tactics. At a time when graft in city governments was reaching new depths, he spent $20 million of public money on public works and never stole a dollar for himself. Still, he broke the city's bank and was effectively thrown out of office when the Senate refused to confirm his new appointment by the President. He defiantly marched off to Mexico, tried his hand at mining gold and silver, and made another fortune for himself.

Shepherd's orgy of modernizing left chaos in his wake, in part because he worked almost at random. Uninterested in tidy, systematic order (or engineering studies), he had proceeded as he saw fit, building streets here and sewers there, consequently leaving to his successors the expensive work of linking up piecemeal improvements. The upshot left the city treasury bankrupt, and angry legislators in the Capitol had to bail out the capital. Partly in retribution, Congress rescinded the territorial status, abolished all suffrage for District residents, and put the city under an appointed board of commissioners that lasted for nearly a century. Night fell on self-government in the seat of the democracy, and the city's leaders and citizens turned to other pursuits: socializing, institution-building, philanthropy, and the like. But while it lasted, the city's summer had been wild and fruitful.

Summer brings out the best of playing fountains and people playing by the Lincoln Memorial Reflecting Pool.
Pages 62-63: The 4.2-acre Enid A. Haupt Garden was dedicated in 1987.

Washington in Autumn: Reap as You Sow

The city's fecund summer slid into a rich harvest season almost as if L'Enfant's plan and Shepherd's public works were so much plowing and planting. Even the natural calamity of an exceptional flood had good results. In 1881 the Potomac rose until its waters lapped at the base of Capitol Hill, and Congress finally took steps toward flood control. Marshes lining the river were drained and filled, then a sea wall built. Dredge spoil provided earth for the artificial peninsula of Potomac Park, while the Tidal Basin was built to provide a reservoir that scoured the new Washington Channel twice daily and kept it from silting up. Withal the riverbank was moved three-quarters of a mile to the west and south.

In 1888 the government's threats to relocate beyond the Mississippi were laid to rest for good when the Departments of State, War, and Navy occupied a colossal—at the time the world's largest office building—and expensive new edifice next to the executive mansion. Now called the Executive Office Building, it blocked New York Avenue's path from the river to the White House, just as the Treasury Building had blocked the sweep of Pennsylvania Avenue to the Capitol since Andrew Jackson's day. (Despite the enduring influence of L'Enfant's plan, from time to time it was overlooked for decades at a stretch.)

As the shape of an autumn landscape's horizon changes when the trees lose their leaves, Washington's skyline rapidly remade itself during the last third of the nineteenth century. From the 1860s the Capitol dominated after starting out as two disjointed wings, then gaining a low center, sprouting outer wings, and finally raising its great dome. By the '80s the steep-towered main building of Georgetown University arose overlooking the Potomac, and the Washington Monument recovered from its false start to reach its peak. In the '90s a new post office building (now inevitably called the Old Post Office) began towering over Pennsylvania Avenue at Eleventh Street, containing a sorting room that was the largest enclosed space in town.

In that decade, too, the miracle of steel-beam architecture lifted the breathtaking Cairo Hotel at Sixteenth and Q Streets NW to a height of 14 stories and 165 feet, beyond the reach of firemen's ladders and also exceed-

A jetliner rises from National Airport across the Potomac. Inset: Fall color highlights benches near the Lincoln Memorial. Pages 66-67: The Chesapeake & Ohio Canal towpath, now the spine of a 185-mile national park, serves hikers, bikers, birders, and Sunday strollers.

ing the bounds of good taste according to many. Citizens raised a ruckus that in time resulted in the imposition of height limits so that few buildings could be taller than 110 feet. Thus Washington would be spared domination by skyscrapers that were turning other cities into mazes of man-made canyons.

To the west and farther uptown, the late nineteenth century also saw Washington gain a new gentry to an unprecedented degree. People of means discovered the city's charms, then in turn charmed others into settling here for a formal social "season" pegged to Congress' calendar. Politicians animated the scene and made themselves accessible to the influential laymen who enriched it. As more wealthy newcomers arrived, they attracted more peers until a province of grand houses spread out from the nexus of Connecticut and Massachusetts Avenues, a neighborhood made especially ripe for chic settlement by Shepherd's works and up-to-date public utilities.

The towering château at Massachusetts and Florida Avenues was built by a retired Civil War naval officer, who was reputedly rich enough to live anywhere. August Miller and his wife chose Washington because it had become "the most beautiful city in the world" and a center of the "culture of the United States." Major D. Clinch Phillips, a glass manufacturer, and his wife, a steel heiress, left

Dupont Circle, hub of the "millionaire colony" early in this century, became a hippy haven in the 1960s, and now serves workers and idlers. The fountain that replaced namesake Rear Adm. Samuel Francis Dupont's statue in 1922 is the work of sculptor Daniel Chester French.

The bronze statue by Frederick Hart at the Vietnam Veterans Memorial on the Mall shows wary soldiers, like the nation itself about that war. Opposite: Across the river near Arlington National Cemetery, the Marine Corps War Memorial boasts larger-than-life Marines raising the flag on Iwo Jima.

Pittsburgh's frigid winters on doctor's orders and tried out Washington in balmy 1896. They soon built a house that their son Duncan Phillips would transform by the 1920s into a gemlike museum, the Phillips Collection.

A new form of extravagant residence appeared as apartment houses competed for the honors of having the most lavish interiors and most Parisian facades. The McCormick on Massachusetts Avenue (now headquarters of the National Trust for Historic Preservation) boasted a silver vault in every butler's pantry, a wall safe in every master bedroom closet, and a corridor 110 feet long. The yearly rent for the 10,000-square-foot top floor flat was twice the salary of its tenant, the Secretary of the Treasury.

America's rising stature in the world was contributing to Washington's ascension as a grand city in its finer precincts. Now its champions awarely set out to make it great. One impetus for this was an aghast reaction against what had come to pass along the once-dreamed "Grand Avenue." There had been a vain effort to adorn this stretch as a series of gardens in the 1850s, when green spaces such as parks (and cemeteries) were planted in many American cities. But that movement had been eclipsed in the next decade as the Civil War stockyards came to surround the unfinished Washington Monument, as railway depots arose and rail yards spread at the foot of Capitol Hill, as clutter increased around a bog called Foggy Bottom, and in general the ugliness of the city proliferated—as it had in most industrial cities of the period.

By contrast, a fantastic vision of a "White City" was glimpsed in Chicago on the shore of Lake Michigan during the World's Columbian Exposition of 1893—a fabulous

The Franciscan
Monastery near
Catholic University
has been a training
ground for missionaries
to the Middle East since
1897. Visitors are wel-
come to stroll through
the Monastery's
gardens and grounds.

Chartered by Congress in 1893, the Washington National Cathedral's (the Cathedral of St. Peter and St. Paul) first chapel was dedicated in 1912, its choir and sanctuary in 1932, and its nave in 1976. The last stone was set atop its south tower in 1990.

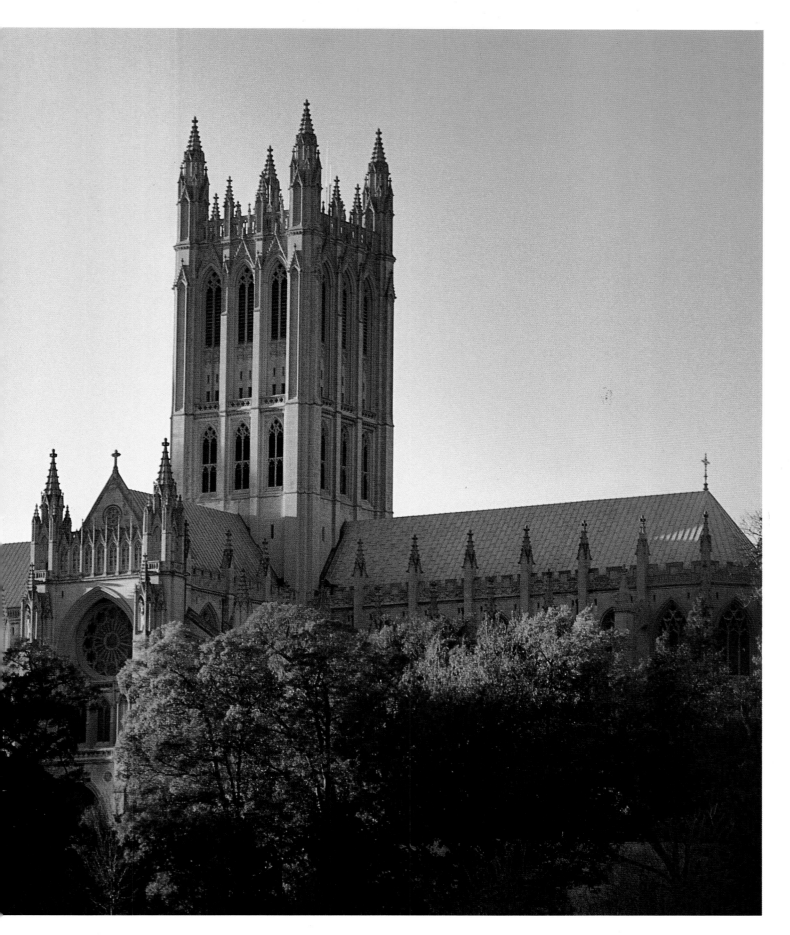

temporary city, a shining fantasy of perfect urbanity. This led to a national craze, the quest for the "City Beautiful" and the movement of that name, which had perhaps its most direct and longevous application in Washington. Here the phenomenon centered on that neglected feature of L'Enfant's plan, the greensward running from the Capitol past the Washington Monument to the Potomac River—what would become universally known as the Mall.

The Chicago Exposition was planned by men who believed in urban planning as a cure for urban ills, and they favored classical forms of buildings. When Daniel Burnham accepted the presidency of the American Institute of Architects in Washington in 1894, he brought with him an agenda for the capital. By 1901 this agenda was endorsed by Senator James McMillan, chairman of the Senate committee that oversaw the affairs of the District. In time to mark the centennial of the capital's birth, McMillan appointed a commission to study the city's land use, a body comprising Burnham, the architect Charles McKim, the landscape designer Frederick Law Olmsted, Jr. (whose father designed New York's Central Park and the Capitol grounds), and the sculptor Augustus Saint-Gaudens.

The McMillan Commission visited Williamsburg, Virginia's colonial capital which featured a mile-long axis with another intersecting it at right angles. (It had been preserved by a century of decline after the state government moved to Richmond.) The commissioners also toured the great capitals and estates of Europe: Paris, Rome, Vienna, Versailles, and Hampton Court. They came home rededicated to the principle of reviving a classical idea: L'Enfant's original plan for Washington's monumental and governmental center. Indeed, the Commission went further by proposing a cruciform layout of parklands and government buildings centered on the Washington Monument. Its short axis ran from the White House south across reclaimed marshlands to the Potomac a mile and a half away; its long axis ran west from the Capitol to the river.

The restored home of
Frederick Douglass in
Anacostia honors the
memory of a man who
was born into slavery,
then found freedom
to become an orator,
abolitionist leader,
and inspiration to
African Americans.

This grove of sandstone columns stands on the grounds of the U.S. National Arboretum, where they were placed in 1989 after being removed from the East Front of the Capitol during the Eisenhower administration.

Some recommendations and much of the Commission's clout were lost in a series of squabbles with and among members of Congress. But its vision for the Mall survived—the vestige of L'Enfant's Grand Avenue. This remnant might be even grander than first planned; certainly it was longer since the Potomac had been pushed back by dredging and filling after the flood of 1881.

The McMillan Plan proposed to encircle the Capitol and White House with government office buildings, an eventuality that has since come to pass more by chance than design. It advocated the development of Arlington National Cemetery and called for federal buildings to line the Mall, which would be dedicated for use as a people's park. Finally, this body's eminence led to the creation of both a Parks Commission that would oversee parklands throughout the area and an authoritative Fine Arts Commission to advise "upon subjects within the domain of the fine arts," especially architecture in the central parts of town.

Under the plan, the Arlington National Cemetery gained prestige. When the Tomb of the Unknown Soldier was dedicated in 1921, so many people lined up for the event—in that newly popular conveyance, the motor car— that a four-hour traffic jam ensued. This so riled members of Congress who had to wait it out that money was appropriated for a new

Potomac River span. Memorial Bridge would link up with the site of another epochal construction, the Lincoln Memorial, which was dedicated in 1922 on land reclaimed from the river.

The first step in clearing the Mall required the removal of railway depots and railroad tracks. Burnham persuaded Pennsylvania Railroad President Alexander Cassatt (expa-

triate painter Mary Cassatt's brother) to move his yards and station, sweetening the kitty with the promise of a consolidated new station nearer to the Capitol and serving several railroads. It was Burnham then who designed Union Station, which was quickly recognized as both an efficient public facility and a paradigm of neoclassical design.

As the Mall was cleared and planted, its border, the old Canal and before that Tiber Creek, would become the route of an imposing Constitution Avenue. (It bears mention that these noble goals were all set aside for a

The city's tallest building, now the Old Post Office, houses small federal agencies and shops. Above: The President's residence became the "White House" when painted to cover fire damage from the War of 1812. The President's Park was renamed Lafayette for the French hero of our Revolution.

81 ◆

time, as World War I came to preoccupy official Washington. The federal establishment made a quantum leap in size to sustain the war effort, and thousands of government offices came to be housed in "temporary" buildings along the Mall, many of which belied their names and remained in use until the 1950s.)

Around the century's turn, neoclassicism was the preferred style of grand architecture in America, and examples of its many forms appeared all over town from the drawing boards of such architects as McKim, Stanford White, and, most notably, John Russell Pope, who built dozens of grand residences and organization buildings. Neoclassicism was not restricted to mimicry of one form, as its most prolific exponent proved. Pope built variously in the styles of ancient Babylon, Egypt, Greece, and Rome, as well as in the Gothic and Georgian idioms.

Its role in commerce withering like an autumn leaf, the waterway of the Potomac now serves mostly recreational purposes such as pleasure boating in vessels from small cruise ships to racing shells.

In Washington the dean of neoclassicists had designed a pair of mansions on Meridian Hill, the National Christian Church at Thomas Circle, the Scottish Rite Masonic Temple on Sixteenth Street, a residence that would house the Audubon Society, another that would become a national lobbyist's headquarters, a war monument, DAR Constitution Hall, and the Jefferson Memorial. He was so active here that some critics held him personally responsible for the city's abundant white-marble look.

By the 1920s plans were laid for neoclassicism to reach a certain pinnacle in the

largest single architectural undertaking ever attempted. It was, said the chairman of the Fine Arts Commission, "the greatest group of public buildings ever constructed at one time in the history of the world." This was the Federal Triangle, a project conceived by AIA President Milton B. Medary and spearheaded by Secretary of the Treasury Andrew Mellon, a multimillionaire investment banker and one of the richest men in America.

President Coolidge proposed the Federal Triangle project in 1923, saying: "If our country wishes to compete with others, let it not be in the support of armaments but in the making of a beautiful Capital City. Let it express the soul of America. Whenever an American is at the seat of his Government, however traveled or cultured a person he may be, he ought to find a city of stately proportion, symmetrically laid out and adorned with the best that there is in architecture, which would arouse his imagination and stir his patriotic pride." As well it might. The nation then had a population of 120 million; at $116,346,472, the project would cost nearly a buck a head.

The project's public champion, Secretary of the Treasury Mellon, saw it restoring the entire city. He forecast that the "Mall will present the spectacle of a great park bordered on one side by the new boulevard [Constitution Avenue] lined with beautiful buildings, and on the other side by a wide park-way of greensward with its four rows of trees, its drives and walks, statues and reflecting pools, all arranged in such a way that long vistas will be

The Capitol surmounts Jenkins Hill surrounded by landscaping designed by Frederick Law Olmsted. The building itself was erected in stages: first the indented wings, then the central section under a low dome, then the exterior wings, and finally the tall, cast-iron dome.

opened up for views of the Capitol in one direction and the Lincoln Memorial in the other....So long as [Washington] remains chiefly a seat of government, it will retain its unique character among the cities of the country. More and more it will be visited by people who will go to Washington because of its beauty and their feeling of pride and personal ownership in the nation's Capital...We do it well, therefore, to give it that beauty and dignity to which it is entitled. In doing so we are not only carrying out those plans which [George] Washington made so long ago for the city which he founded but, at the same time, we are justifying that faith which he had from the beginning in the future greatness of America."

Bounded by Fourteenth Street, Pennsylvania Avenue, and Constitution Avenue,

the Federal Triangle covered twenty-seven acres with twelve enormous buildings, enough to house most of the 60,000 civil servants then working in Washington. Rather than give the single project to one architect, Mellon appointed a committee of the nation's most successful names; together they worked out a set of standards for the complex, then parcelled out separate buildings for each member of the select group to design. The overall scheme called for unifying features: cornices, at the same height, roofs of the same red tiles, and facades of the same buff stone. All the buildings would be neoclassical in appearance. If the buildings of the Federal Triangle seemed so impressive in their individual and collective scale as to be almost forbidding, that was not by accident. Rather than warmly welcome citizens, they were intended to impress

Opening in 1971, the white marble John F. Kennedy Center for the Performing Arts brings new distinction to Washington by providing fine stages for music, theater, and dance. A year later in the curved Watergate office complex, a burglary led to the resignation of President Nixon. These buildings climax the physical growth of Washington by completing the ceremonial riverfront. Pages 88-89: The city's busiest corner on Saturday nights and whenever a local pro sports team wins a championship is where L'Enfant never would have guessed: in Georgetown at the intersection of Wisconsin Avenue and M Street.

all comers with the grandeur of government.

After Mellon left government, he gave Washington one of its most important embellishments in what would become one of its most enduring attractions. He personally chose its site: across Constitution Avenue from the flatiron building at the Federal Triangle's eastern apex (the Federal Trade Commission) and a block east of John Russell Pope's contribution to the Triangle, the National Archives Building. Creating a special hybrid of private beneficence and governmental stewardship, Mellon gave to the nation the National Gallery of Art, a pink marble temple to art that Pope designed as his masterpiece and swan song.

Mellon hatched a plan and struck an agreement with President Franklin Roosevelt who sold it to Congress. The private patron agreed to donate his world-class collection of Old Master paintings along with a suitable building to shelter and display them to the public free of charge; the Federal government in turn agreed to maintain the building and grounds in perpetuity, providing staff from gardeners and guards to curators. Thanks to Mellon's original gift and to even greater generosity from his two children, Ailsa Mellon Bruce and Paul Mellon, thanks also to deft leadership and the good fortune of lavish acquisitions, the National Gallery of Art became one of the great museums in the world within the remarkably short span of a few decades.

And so on the eve of World War II, with the addition of the National Gallery crowning fifty years of remarkable growth, the city itself joined the first rank of world capitals.

Winter: Coming to the Cusp

Since before the city's beginning, winters at this latitude have been bland, bright, or brought extremes in sharp doses. The first example of the latter came in December 1799, when George Washington, living a vigorous retirement at Mount Vernon in his sixty-eighth year, returned home from riding in a snowstorm, took to his bed with laryngitis, and died two days later—barely a fortnight before the turn of the century and the coming of the New Year that would see his namesake city become the capital.

In this century wintertime has brought results every bit as tragic and others simply disappointing. In 1922, for example, a two-foot snowfall collapsed the roof of the Knickerbocker Theater, killing nearly a hundred moviegoers. In 1961 it snowed abundantly on the eve of John F. Kennedy's inauguration, so heavily that at first it snarled traffic and then paralyzed the city as few guests could reach the sites of inaugural balls and others were stranded all over town. A few years later the winter stayed so cold for so long that the Potomac froze bank-to-bank, thick enough for ice-skating, bonfires, and other horseplay on the ice. In 1985 for Ronald Reagan's glittery second inaugural, daytime temperatures hovering near zero forced the cancellation of the inaugural parade lest marchers freeze and spectators get frostbite or worse. In other winters here, the weather has stayed mild as milk toast.

Washington's symbolic year started coming full circle a century and a half after the District of Columbia was founded and L'Enfant put plan on paper. Its figurative winter started around 1940—if winter may be seen (as it is by farmers or naturalists) as a time of retrenchment, transitions, and preparation for burgeoning spring. When the pall of World War II began to fall, the "tempo" office buildings built to serve World War I were not only still present, they had multiplied for the second conflict, uglified the Mall even more, and deterred further the fulfillment of that greensward's promise. The population of the city swelled, as it had for the Great and Civil Wars; transportation slowed to a crawl (hampered by congestion, if not by artillery wagons breaking the pavement). Housing was not quite as scarce as in the early years when Congressmen bunked together in rooming houses, but it pushed people to acts of bizarre ingenuity.

Foliage at Tudor Place is weighted by a wet snow. Opposite: Pierce Mill grinds grist again in Rock Creek Park—a historical model recalling the time when water power was a key source of energy.

Apartments were so hard to find that would-be renters bought black-market proof sheets of obituary pages from newspaper press rooms to get word early of newly vacated digs.

If Washington could survive the perils of this season, it would be on the verge of a flowering that would place it among the great capitals of the world. Nay, if the world could survive, for this was the war that loosed nuclear weapons upon the planet and ended in little more than a bilateral standoff that would fray global nerves for nearly half a century.

In 1940, Mr. and Mrs. Robert Woods Bliss relinquished their Georgetown house and gardens to the stewardship of Harvard University, which would see it used for both belligerent causes and hopeful, peaceful ones. Built around the turn of the eighteenth century, "Oakly" had been John C. Calhoun's home, the place where the great orator played host and bon vivant in pursuit of the presidency. Now, for some twenty years, the Blisses had been creating a rare and complex amenity, a country home in a capital city, a treasury of art surrounded by formal gardens unsurpassed on this continent for ordered vitality and grace. When what they called Dumbarton Oaks ceased to be their home, it became a museum for their collections of Byzantine and pre-Columbian art, as well as a conference center. Here plans were laid to develop the atomic bomb, and later the idea of the United Nations would be born at a 1944 conference.

In 1940 on Mount Saint Alban the Washington National Cathedral—now only

Frigid moonlight illuminates a neoclassical profile of the National Gallery of Art's West Building, the edifice that brought world-class art to Washington.

fractionally completed—was designated the seat of the Presiding Bishop of the Episcopal Church. Its visionary plans made it out to be the sixth largest gothic cathedral in the world—a thirteen-story building could stand in its nave—and a surrogate for L'Enfant's once-vaunted pantheon downtown. For now, as Dickens once saw this city lack only "houses, roads, and inhabitants," this sanctuary lacked only a nave, transept, and spires to be a towering cathedral as it attempted to serve the spirit of a nation going to war.

In 1940 the city's population had grown to some 663,091, an increase of one-third in ten years after a previous gain by one-third the decade before. In the next ten years the number of inhabitants would leap again to peak at more than 800,000—thus having doubled in size within one generation. Then it began to lose residents decade by decade, though the city was not losing size or prominence. Rather, Washington was becoming the capital of a region as well as a nation, the heart of a metropolis that was spreading throughout the surrounding ring of rural counties, which would become suburban and even urban themselves. By now Washington was the heart of a "standard metropolitan area" (in Census Bureau terms) that would reach out for fifty miles and within half a century claim a gross population approaching 10 million.

By 1941, the year the National Gallery opened and the year Japan attacked the U.S.

The North Portico is the ceremonial entrance to a White House that has been enlarged by more than one hundred rooms since Abigail Adams kept house there as first First Lady. Its original 1792 design, by James Hoban, was based on the Dublin home of an English duke.

fleet at Pearl Harbor, the Jefferson Memorial was under construction on the south side of the Tidal Basin, completing that useful reservoir's charm and complementing the springtime beauty of its exotic flowering cherry trees. The building that gracefully recalled Jefferson's home Monticello (which had in turn echoed Rome's Pantheon) had been the cause of loud and noisy conflict. First there were voices raised against the late John Russell Pope's design, saying he had already raised one templelike dome over the Gallery on the Mall. Then a group of genteel ladies demonstrated against the Memorial's construction because it would mean sacrificing some of the famous cherry trees. These had been championed by Mrs. William Howard Taft as first lady and received by the nation as a gift of friendship from a foreign nation; rather than let them be cut down to make way for the building, the ladies chained themselves for the span of a morning to the cherry trees. The trees' Japanese origin would be politely and patriotically ignored for some springs to come.

In 1942 work began on the Pentagon across the Potomac in Arlington. This construction was so rushed that the building was started before the architectural drawings were finished. Completed in a year, what remains the world's largest office building was one mile in circumference and boasted seventeen miles of corridors as well as one of the nation's first interior shopping complexes. Perhaps this would become its most long-lived contribu-

tion to the commonweal—the indoor shopping mall.

In short, the war years brought a variety of qualitative changes to Washington as well as the expected quantitative ones, and when World War II ended (as the Cold War began), those changes accelerated. Stark architecture, inspired at first by the German-born Bauhaus school, had come into vogue with the demise of neoclassicism in the late 1930s, which coincided with John Russell Pope's death in 1937. The next few decades would see the proliferation of unornamented buildings— egg-crates and blocks of concrete, glass, and steel such as would transform K Street, for example, into a grim corridor cutting through the downtown business district. The rise of the high-rise would likewise turn the Virginia shoreline facing Washington into a futuristic forest of high density development complete with copses of offices and residential towers.

Closer to home, and closer in spirit at

Washington National Cathedral is the world's sixth largest gothic building. Above: Artisans' masterpieces grace it in materials from stone to embroidery, including this iron vignette of Abraham and Isaac. Pages 98-99: A dusting of snow lends form to flying buttresses.

The Jefferson Memorial graces a key site on land created since the founders' time by dredging the Potomac. Despite loud opposition, President Roosevelt approved the Memorial on the eve of World War II, as Lincoln had finished the Capitol dome in wartime. Opposite: The bronze statue of the nation's third president is the work of sculptor Rudolph Evans.

least to L'Enfant's plan, the Mall in particular gained an impressive collection of buildings—impressive at least for their contents and their programs. Powered by yet another dynamo who would leave his mark on Washington, the Smithsonian Institution experienced its greatest period of growth since its founding with the installation of S. Dillon Ripley as its eighth secretary. An ornithologist by training, Ripley emerged from academia to take over the "Castle" as certainly as a migrating blue jay arrives in his old tree and claims his breeding territory.

The Smithsonian had long been called the "nation's attic," because people perceived that it functioned largely in the manner of a Victorian museum, collecting millions of things of every description and more

or less setting out a few thousand examples on dusty display for the public to view. It was a research institution as well, in particular a world science center for the classification of plants and animals, and also a community of scholars studying myriad aspects of history and technology. In any case, all these activities required space and facilities, especially as science and scholarship increased, and as the nature of museums changed—with the Smithsonian in the van—to actively attract more of the public inside with increasingly dynamic exhibits and programs.

Not only that, there were more museums in the offing to augment the "Castle," its original adjunct the Arts & Industries Building (built to house exhibits saved from Philadelphia's Centennial Exposition of 1876), and the National Museum of Natural History, a turn-of-the-century mausoleum on the north side of the Mall. By the time Ripley was done he had expanded the Smithsonian to include the Hirschhorn Museum and Sculpture Garden, the Air & Space Museum (said to be the most popular in the world), the Arthur M. Sackler Gallery, an expanded Freer Gallery with its special collections of Asian art, and a growing National Museum of African Art. Like the city itself, this community of museums was growing to rival its older peers around the world.

Overlooking the Potomac just upstream from the Mall arose another institution of national importance, which came to be named for one of its political sponsors, the John F.

Kennedy Center for the Performing Arts. Washington had been a theater town for a century or more and recently had sustained Arena Stage, one of the nation's first successful professional repertory companies. Downtown still boasted the National Theater, which presented many notable world premieres of plays on their way to Broadway, including *Show Boat* in the roaring '20s and *Hello, Dolly* to end the period of public mourning after President Kennedy's death. Now Washington gained a single complex of presenting halls—a major stage plus space for experimental and intimate theaters including cinemas, restaurants, an opera house, and a concert hall that would be the home of the National Symphony Orchestra. This ensemble, which had struggled bravely for three decades since its founding by Hans Kindler, soon attracted a conductor of international distinction, Antal Dorati, and then a maestro of world eminence in Russian-born cellist and composer Mstislav Rostropovich.

The capital in the '50s and '60s also saw a thriving visual arts community, notably painters of the "Washington color school" such as Gene Davis, Morris Louis, Kenneth Noland, and Jacob Kainen. There was also a flock of natural scientists passing through, including Roger Tory Peterson, who practically invented the practical field guide for birders and plant stalkers, and Louis Halle, author of the classic *Spring in Washington*, who aptly wrote: "The city of Washington has never had the praise it deserves from those of us who

At Dumbarton Oaks, light snow outlines promises of spring. Dedicated to scholarly use, it proved an 1847 newspaper's claim: "If there be one question set to rest in this community, it is that public opinion has decided that the national metropolis shall be distinguished for the cultivation of the mind."

◆ 102

Bouquets, flags, letters, and memorabilia adorn the Vietnam Veterans Memorial wall of names and the nearby statue; the dozens of tributes left daily are collected, catalogued, and stored by the U.S. Park Service. Opposite: The eloquent design of the memorial by Yale student Maya Ying Lin, one of 1,421 submitted, features an inscribed wall of black granite, its two wings pointing to the Washington Monument and the Lincoln Memorial.

do not give ourselves altogether to city life...It makes room for nature in its midst and seems to welcome it." Another local writer Rachel Carson, a career biologist at the U.S. Fish and Wildlife Service, found readers the world over, first by charming them with the miracles of nature in *The Sea Around Us*. Later she awakened America to impending ecological disaster in *Silent Spring*, the environmental clarion and one of the epochal books of our apocalyptic century.

The 1960s also saw the best and worst of the civil-rights movement. President Harry Truman had desegregated the armed forces in 1948, and the integration movement had been gathering steam ever since, as schools and public accommodations began dropping the color bar. In 1963 Washington hosted a unique event; civil-rights leaders and ordinary citizens from all over the country gathered in behalf of new proposals. They set

out to petition Congress, and their numbers swelled so that when speeches began on the Lincoln Memorial steps, people filled the area in front and spread along each side of the Reflecting Pool for its entire length.

This was the first of the huge demonstrations that would continue throughout the decade—initially for civil rights, then in a somehow kindred effort to protest the increasingly unpopular war in Vietnam. The era of the "global village" had begun, and Washington had become the town square where citizens congregated in times of community crisis.

In 1968 the civil rights leader Rev. Dr. Martin Luther King, Jr. was slain, and thousands of African Americans in cities across the country took to the streets in violent reaction, rioting and looting. Here they burned several commercial areas which would hardly be rebuilt in the course of a generation. However, one street would be renovated and another invented.

Pennsylvania Avenue, not the victim of rioters but of neglect, had become a drab byway lined with cheap hotels and liquor stores. When England's King and Queen visited, every paper in the country reported that they had to pass tattoo parlors to reach the White House. When World War II broke out, a USO canteen opened on the street linking the Congress' house with the President's. Thus, President Lyndon Johnson created the Pennsylvania Avenue Development Corporation, which combined governmental catalysts with private cooperation to mobilize the

WM T LAFIELD Jr · MICHAEL W HILL
E SLAGOWSKI · NAZIR MOHAMMED
ARTON S CREED · NEAL S CROWDER
EDDIE W VENCILL · JAMES C WARD
CO DIPHILLIPO · BOBBY JENE FIELDS
ACK D MO... · RANDY M RIGSBY
W STEWART · MARCUS S STOEN
JOHN E LAM... · PATRICK D ERB
E M HARR... · PHILIP R JAMROCK
SON ...GREGORY S MORGAN
HARD... · DAVID M SEXTON
EL... · JAMES L GETTER
BERT... RAYMOND J SAATHOFF
MICHAEL J S DEPAC... CRAIG M DIX
CE L ILLY · WILLIAM C NEWBOULD
OUGLAS M SELLEY · BRYANT SUTTON
ETT A BRANDT · JOHN R CHAMPLIN
MARTINEZ GARCIA · JON M SPARKS
TON L WOOLRIDGE · JACK E BARKER
IAM E DILLENDER · JOHN E DUGAN
T C MAURO Jr · ROBERT... MARTIN Jr
S D SCHOOLEY · JOHN... RIESDELL
ST L HIRTLER · DAVID... ...CASTER
CLAUDIUS A SM... · ...E B TIMS
RRY W DOAN · KAR... ...ZEWSKI
PHEN D GUC...SKI · WALTER R H...
OME E LE ROY · LARRY D...
MCLEMORE Jr · ROGER...
OMAS L ZEIGLER · SH... ...VANT
NNIS M HOTALING · JEF... KETTLE...
ILLIAM L SCHELL · WARREN P SEA...
Y M BECKWITH III · DAVID L COKER Jr
WILLIAM E NEAL · HERMAN E PICHON
M STONE · WILLIAM F THOMPSON Jr
D KEALOHA RAMOS · EDDIE L DODD
DA· DOYLE FOSTER · GARY G GEIGER
D McDONELL · JEFFREY M PARMELEE
E JACKSON · RANDALL A THOMPSON
· ROBERT D COFFEY · JAY J FISHBECK
CE R KISELEWSKI · DEAN W KRUEGER
RY A SCHULTZ · GORDON E TIBBETTS
TT BRADLEY · ROBERT C CHAUDOIN
LSON · PAUL E SERVEN · GLEN H YELL...
D C BENNETT · VICTOR R BENNETT Jr
CLIFFORD W CORR · LARRY D AUSTIN
RUEY LEE HATFIELD · JOHN L HOGAN
RICHARD V KNIGHT Jr · LARRY P LAND
LAYMON PALMER · STEVEN D PLATH
DALLAS D ROBINSON · PAUL A SHEER
ALD M STOTTS · ROGER D WHIRLOW
NT D ERICKSON · MICHAEL A FRATTALI
ROGER A PEDERSON · BARRY A RHASH...
ALLEN E KINSMAN · JAMES H ALLEN
AMADO ALANIZ Jr · DAVID F NIDEVER
ICHAEL A WADE · MICHAEL A YOUNG
DOLPH L MARTHE · HAROLD E MYERS
JAMES SALLEY · GUY G SHANNON Jr
HARRIS L WILLIAMS · JAMES A HIGHSMITH
JR HERNANDEZ · JAMES A HIGHSMITH
WRAY · GEORGE M YOUNGERMAN
HERLAND · JOSEPH M BOWER Jr
R BOROWSKI · HOWARD A THOMASON
BERT J KISER · KENNETH O WARBINGTON
TRUJILLO · HOWARD W HOMSCHEK
NNY E HART · ROBERT W... JOSEPH S SMITH
ARVEY M REYNOLDS · KARL R BERBERT...
R ALEXANDER · ARTHUR GLASS

PHILIP C BLACKMOND · PHEN J HADLEY · ALLEN D SCOGGIN · B DEWINE · JAMES R COOPER · GEORGE D CHRISS · LEWIS C QUIROZ
JOB NAVARRETE Jr · ARTHUR C STEPHENS Jr · CHARLES T MEADOWS · HOWARD WILLIAMS · PHILLIP S GLASS · GUY W WINKLES Jr · CHRIS B CORDORA
DALE A PEARCE · DONALD O CARTER · DAVID R WINKEL · THOMAS E STEVEN C BURNS · SAM HOLMES Jr
LARRY J GAMMON · LARRY LEE ROBINSON · WAYNE R WILLIAMS · CHARLES L MARTIN · LAWRENCE E GARCIA S
HERBERT S BARNES · WILLIAM M GEORGE · DAVID P SOYLAND · THOMAS KUKOWSKI · LEONARD M WINTERS
JAMES D AGUILAR · ROBERT G BRUCE · PHILIP R DEARING · DALE W DEHNKE · DANNY D YOSHONIS
GREGORY A SMITH · MARCUS E ARNESON · LOWELL F GLOSSUP · MIKLE E DIXON · JAMES E TORRENCE · RICHARD J ENTRICAN
CHARLES M CRAWFORD · ALVIN C CURRY · VINCENT M BENEDETTI · SCOTT K NEWPORT · TERRANCE R SCHENE
COLUMBUS V GROSS · BILLY D HERRING · THOMAS F DELEHANT · RANDALL J GLASSPOOLE · HAROLD D WALLER
WILLIAM M KENEDY · CHARLES N KOWALK · WILLIAM H HJORTH · JOE F GAYOSSO · JAMES E BODDIE
STEVEN M MITCHELL · JOHN H NAJMOLA · KARL J LAVALLEE · WILLIAM C JENNINGS · CHRISTOPHER J BIGLEY
OSIER L PRUITT · ALBERTO A RAMIREZ · JAMES E TIGHE · ROBERT B LE CATES · BILLY JOE JAMES
GEORGE T TAYLOR Jr · BENNIE LEE NORTH · KENNETH G WESTERBERG · WILLIAM SAYLOR Jr · LEO C OATMAN · DAVID B MATYKIEWICZ
GARY A DORE · THOMAS R LUSHER · EDWARD W METCALF · WILLIAM T SMITH · JEROME A OLSON
RALPH E POSEY · ROY G SHADDON · PATRICK WEBER · WILLIAM E WOLFE · J C SUMMERLIN
TOM R ADLER · JOHN H GRUBER · JAMES W PETERSON · RICHARD J PLU...
LARRY R DEWEY · JIMMY D HUMPHRES · RANDALL C SHORT · ARMANDO MARIN ZEPEDA · HENRY D...
WILLIAM E ADAMS · JOHN D CURRAN · GERALD M LUBBEHUSEN · PHILIP D SHARP · ROBERT K BREWSTER
MICHAEL D RIDDLE · MELVIN ROBINSON · DENNIS C DURAND · ROY L MEADOWS · JACKIE DEAN...
HARVEY E HUMPHREY · LEROY J WESTRA · ROY IGNACIO · JOHN W LITTLETON
ROBERT L BROWN · STEPHEN CHAVIRA · PAUL D CARTER · JERRY FOY · THOMAS W KNUCKEY · STEVEN W...
THOMAS G BLAIR Jr · STEPHEN G DAVIES · JOSEPH D ESPARZA · DONALD W KNUCKEY · PHILIP C HICKS
ROBERT K CAIN II · ERVIN B CHERRY · JOSEPH E SWEENEY · JOSE MARIA R ARREDONDO · PAUL D URQU...
STEVEN J KEARNS · CLINTON A MUSIL Sr · GARY J SHINN · MITCHELL O BARNES · ROY M SEABROOK · WAYNE...
DEAN R ISAACS · LEON J JACKSON · GARY L SHINN · AUGUSTUS ADAMS · GEORGE...
ROBERT D McKINNEY · DON M RAMSEY · PAUL G MAGERS · DENNIS L MEDUNA
DONALD J WANN · SCOTT W WAYT · JAMES R SAXON · ANDREW C STRO...
ROBERT P SANCHEZ Jr · MICHAEL A LAMUSGA · EDWARD A WERMAN · KEVIN...
TERRY BRIGGS · RANDALL J BOYD · GEORGE H POTTS · EDGAR D TH... · DANNY R KING
JAMES W MYL... · FRANCISCO TORRES-RAMOS · JOSE ANGEL SANCHEZ · DAN... · MICHAEL VERSTRAETE
LARRY LEE MILLER · DAVIS J MORGAN · LEM CLARK · JOHN R...
HAROLD E BARNARD · CARL W BORCHERS · WILLIAM K TAYLOR · BILLY H...
THOMAS E BAUMGAR... Jr · DAVID C BROWN · MARTIN F LOVING · MICHAEL...
THOMAS H FARMER · HIAWATHA H WILLIAMS · ANTHONY M EILERS · JERRY...
MICHAEL M DALTON · HUGH A SEXTON Jr · JOHN R MICKLE · THOMAS...
...MONTOYA · WILLIAM C BILL... · ROBERT L SIMMONS · JOHNNY ARTHUR · CARL W BREWSTER
THOMAS W BEATTY · CARROLL... · THOMAS J CONNIFF · JOHNNY JACKSON · LOYD E ROBINSON
RICHARD J GRAY · JOSEPH HAYES · RALPH L CHURCH · GARY L PFLASTER · STEVEN J ELLIS
LEONARD L BROENNEKE · FRANKLIN T CRITES · JAMES D JACKSON · CHARLES A SANCHEZ · GARY L WESTPHAL
MANUEL... DAV... ANTHON... · DENNIS M DICKE · JEFFREY D SCHUMACHER · EARL R LESTER Jr
FLOYD L BRADSHAW... ...ESTER C MARTINEZ · ...PRICE · WAYNE A GARBER · WILLIAM T WALSH · DEE BERGERA
DONA... THOMA... HARVEY · BILLY D PEDINGS · JAMES A SOUTHER · RICHARD WILSON Jr
...DAVID... CURTIS · DANNY D STUDDARD · ERNEST K TYLER · JAMES R VALTR...
PHILL... WRIGHT · ERNEST D HART Jr · HAROLD E IMLER Jr · TERRY L KELLY
PHIL... GARY L JOHNSON · LARRY A BIDWELL · RAYMOND V DEBLASIO Jr · JOHN T DOZIER II
...W FITCHETT · JOHN R PAINTER Jr · WILLIAM E REED · ROGER E WITTE
DWIGHT T... ...LAGO TEO · JOHN W HAYNES · RANDY V HINES · HOWARD H NELSON
ARTHUR... ...MILLER · JOHNNY SOTO · WHEELER D BROOKS · JOHN E LEIS
ELBERT... ...LUSCOMBE · CHARLES... METZLER · FRANK RODRIQUEZ YBARRA · BILLY JOE WATSON
DONALD... ...MARSHALL G MILLER · MADIS... · EARL W ELLIS · FLOYD W WOODS
...HOLLOWAY · ROBERT EGGLESTON · STROHLEIN · DONNIE W ANDERSON
...MELV... ...ALBERT P CARDEN · GILBERT... MATTHEWS Jr · TOIVO B NOMM
...MORGAN... ...MICHAEL J WHITAKER · CHARLES T JONES · RICHARD N LEE · RUBIN MATHIS II
...SPEIDLE... ...HERBERT J ARTIS · MICHAEL R WILSON · DONALD F McKIETHAN
...STUART M BINKLEY · RICHARD W JONES · CHARLES W COOK
...WILLIE JAM...S Jr · BERNARD F BRZEZINSKI · DARYL W TAYLOR
...TWALTON Jr · LARRY M LIVINGSTON · WILLIAM A WALTERS
...BRIDGES · MASON A LEITH · RONALD H HALL · GERALD C HINSDALE
...HOUSTON · PAULA DODSON Sr · MICHAEL W NICOL · STEVEN C ONEAL
...LAMERE... · GARY L LEWIS · PATRICK B MORRIS · GLEN L FULLERTON
...YINGLING... ...TURNER · DUANE M McBEAIN · DONALD J EVANS
...MURPH... ...FREDDIE C MANN · PHILLIP R BERGFIELD · RICHARD SALLEE II
...MARK RUSSELL... · TERRY JACK MARTELL · VICTOR W LEW...
...FAREWELL... · MANOLO BRIONES AGNES · ISRAEL MEDINA
...TOMLINSON · STEVEN G WILLIAMS · PAUL LOPEZ · ROBERT F DAVIS
...PURCELL · NAPOLEON JOHNSON · GILBERT LEDGER · DANIEL W THOMAS
...RICHARD... ...LAWRENCE WILKERSON · DONALD G CARR · CHARLES J BEALS
...MORTIMER Jr · WINDOL W McNUTT · FREDERICK B SUMMERVILLE · JOHN H MORRIS
...GOFF · RICHARD S PATTERSON · RUBEN RUBIO · CHARLES P PANQUERNE · ROBERT L KING
...ALAN S GOFF · MICHAEL J KNOX · RAYMOND R MAYS · WAYNE C PISCIOTTA · CURTIS G VAN WINKLE
...PAUL R WITHROW · MARION T GRIFFIN · SAMUEL W McDANIEL II · THOMAS W BICKFORD · STEPHEN A BEDNAR
...E BEUTLER · ROBERT J MANTAS · BRYANT WILKEN · LANCE D WORKMAN · TED J TAYLOR
...RONALD E KRIEG · MICHAEL LUKOW · HOWARD J BECKER Jr · ROBERT M LARSON · JAY S ASTON
...THOMAS T COLLINS · WILLIAM ALEXANDER W DUPLESSIE · GREGORY T SAHLBERG · RUDOLPH STEVENS
...DANIEL G DORMAN · ROY D RUSSELL · ALLEN E NOBLE · CHARLES W ROBERTS Jr · GERRY DON COULT...
...MICHAEL WATKINS · JAMES M DICKEY · JOHN LEFTHEROLF · TONY ANGUIANO
...CHRISTOPHER C COOK · JOHN H LOPOCHINSKY · STEVEN MINKLER · ALBERT E PETERSON · CHARLES R HARRI...
...ALLEN J DYER · JAMES D JOHNSON · MARGARITO RODRIGUEZ GOMEZ · STEPHEN E SLOCUM · LINWOOD A GROSS
...JAMES D CHEEK · NORMAN MAXIE · RONALD N GOODWIN · DANNY LEE LIGHTSEY · JOHN A CLARK
...HILBERT... LUIS J... · JIM H TAKETA · CHARLES CLARK
...NELSON... ...CHALSEY YOUNG · RANDALL H GEIS · ALLEN H CLARK

RONALD J BOND
ORVILLE C
PHILIP M
CARL W THOMPSON
CHESTER A LI... ELD
DAVID G SMITHWICK
ANGEL ALARID QUEV...
ROBERT F QU...
JERRY G C...
ARLIE M...
PAUL TRUJILLO...
ROLIN J CROSSI...
EARL E TOM...
HENRY F DELLECKER P...
DANNY T JETT...
HAROLD J RITCH...
VINCENT P MARTIN Jr
CHARLES A POPPLETON
ROBERT R CH...
RONNIE S...
JOHN W GEORGE...
ROBERT D BEUTEL II
JAMES H SPANN · JOSEP...
BILLY RAY COFFEY · HOW...
WILL R...
ARCHIE C...
STEVEN...
OSCAR PAULLEY
WILLIAM D THOMPSON
ROBERT E...
JOE S BURG...
KENNETH R PER...
THOMAS E FIKE · RON...
GEORGE SABLAN MENO...
PHILIP S GALLA...
BERNARD J MORAN Jr
GREGG A...
ANDREW A MESHIGAU...
LEO THO...
RONALD J COLEMAN
VINCENT E GALK...
ROBERT L DEN...
DOUGLAS E TROTTER
MICHAEL SCHMIDT · RAU...
JAMES LOSPINUSO...
KENNETH C WILLIAM...
RICHARD I...
RONALD A LONGFELLOW...
WALTER C B...
MARK E ALLEN...
GREGORY C DAVIS · KURT...
DONALD G BAILEY · DON...
CHARLES E GREENE...
JAMES E M...
JAMES W KIEHNE · R...
ROBERT E PE...
PAUL L...
DON H WAR...
MARK J FITZGERALD · R...
DAVID N JONES...
ROBERT L DALIGHERT...
REGEN A NIONETTE E...
RAYMOND E F...
GEORGE W LINTON...
JOHN M MINOR · R...
COLUMBUS WATSON...
LARRY W HARVEY R...
BILLY R CO...
JOHN L CLARK · JAME...
JAMES AMMO...

refurbishing of Pennsylvania Avenue. One by one the eyesores were removed and replaced, like as not by huge new office buildings; in a few cases by government buildings, and uniquely by the spectacular Canadian Embassy. This bit of foreign domain was allowed to command a matchless view of the Capitol—and to overlook the inaugural parade every four years—in recognition of both the special amity between the two nations and of the fact that the American Embassy in Ottawa overlooks Parliament.

The new artery, the Capital Beltway, was the offspring of President Eisenhower's farthest reaching domestic program, the plan to build interstate highways throughout America. Circling the city about five miles from the center, the Beltway let long-distance travelers and truckers entirely avoid the city while it linked suburbs directly to each other. Consequently, from the 1960s onward, the Washington metropolitan area grew in entirely new patterns and directions thanks to the larger community's new "main street."

Seagulls soar above a puddle's reflection of the ceremonial city's epicenter at the east end of the Mall.

So it was that Washington evolved with the changing times. It had all sorts of residents, from retired congressmen to abstract expressionists, and manifold activities, from bird watching to grand opera. Which was the chicken and which the egg? Government came here certainly in 1800. And with government in time there emerged a community of people, and with them the basis for an economy as goods and services circulated in

*The Lincoln Memorial
anchors the Mall at
its west end on ground
reclaimed from marsh.
Daniel Chester French's
huge statue of Abraham
Lincoln dominates the
Memorial in which one
often hears his whispered
words—as visitors read
aloud inscriptions on
the inner walls.
Pages 110-111: Like
time or history, Rock
Creek passes ceaselessly
despite the concealing
blanket of the season.
Page 112: The
Washington Monument's
cornerstone was laid in
1847 at a ceremony
that a reporter avowed
"surpassed in magnifi-
cence and moral
grandeur anything of
the kind ever witnessed
in this metropolis since
the formation of the
Republic."*

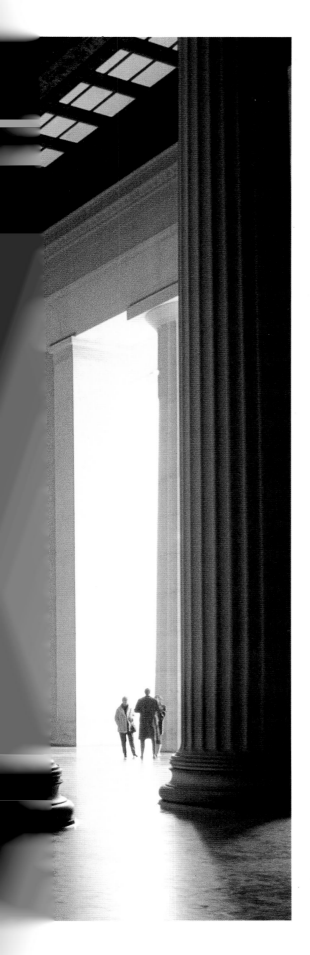

growing amounts and at increasing rates. The nation itself expanded in geographic size, human population, material wealth, and world influence. What all this meant was that at some point in the middle of the twentieth century, Washington achieved critical mass. To use the old cliché, it came of age. To amend L'Enfant's ambition for the city he conceived, it increasingly acquired "that ag-

grandizement and embellishment which the increase of the wealth of the nation [would] permit it to pursue at [every] period however remote."

Planted by cogent choice two centuries ago, nurtured by generations of variously hopeful, energetic, and ambitious people, Washington has come into flower (even as it has grown thorns and raised weeds). Yet at its core as a seat of government, in its centers of learning, within its civilized and cultured heart, it has become a City of Magnificent Realities.